DUMB HUSBANDS

A Play

by

JOHN SHEPHARD

LIST OF CHARACTERS

John Harding
Helen
Jack Brandon
Peter
Adrian
Jennifer
Collins
Amanda Robertson
Frank Robertson

The living room of John's house in North London.

ACT I   Wednesday evening.

ACT II
   Scene One   Friday afternoon.
   Scene Two   That evening.

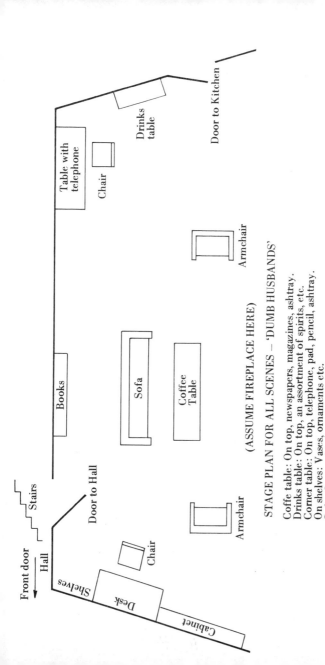

(ASSUME FIREPLACE HERE)

STAGE PLAN FOR ALL SCENES – 'DUMB HUSBANDS'

Coffe table: On top, newspapers, magazines, ashtray.
Drinks table: On top, an assortment of spirits, etc.
Corner table: On top, telephone, pad, pencil, ashtray.
On shelves: Vases, ornaments etc.
Sofa: One cushion.

The Stage for Act II should give a general impression of untidiness compared to Act I.

Labels in diagram:

Front door
Hall
Stairs
Door to Hall
Shelves
Desk
Cabinet
Chair
Armchair
Books
Sofa
Coffee Table
Armchair
Table with telephone
Chair
Drinks table
Door to Kitchen

ACT I

The living room of JOHN'S *house in North London. It is comfortably furnished and decorated with taste but not extravagance.*

Wednesday evening. As the curtain rises JOHN *is sitting on the sofa reading a newspaper and smoking a cigarette. After a few moments,* HELEN *enters from the hall in her dressing gown.*

JOHN: Hello. How was the bath?

HELEN: *(sitting on armchair, right)* Uneventful. And almost hot. You're back early.

JOHN: Yes. I'm afraid the pub these days is full mainly of long haired revolutionaries who drone on permanently and loudly about their profession. Mostly teachers or frustrated sadists, usually both.

HELEN: You're a teacher.

JOHN: Yes, and probably a frustrated sadist as well, but I don't boast about it. *(pause)* Where's Peter?

HELEN: He's gone to a crisis meeting of the Students' Union.

JOHN: What's the crisis? Are they threatening to ban the smoking of marijuana during lectures?

HELEN: He's told you enough times what the crisis is. There's talk of closing the college and handing over the site to the University. I think the Union's planning some sort of action against it. That's what the meeting's for.

JOHN: Oh yes. I do remember some talk of that nature over

breakfast the other day.

HELEN: Actually, Peter did all the talking; you made a pretence at listening.

JOHN: Ah. I take it that he took it that it *was* only a pretence?

HELEN: Well, it was fairly obvious.

JOHN: To you, perhaps . . . . still. *(pause)* You haven't asked me what sort of day I had at school. *(Rises to pour a drink behind the sofa)* Drink?

HELEN: No, thanks. Should I have asked you then?

JOHN: It might be worthwhile, and if nothing else, then polite. *(sitting)*

HELEN: All right. How was your day?

JOHN: Well, actually it started off very strangely. On entering the staff room first thing this morning I was approached, almost attacked in fact, by a zestful chap named Collins — he's a sort of general dogsbody and errand runner masquerading under the title of Social Activities Master — Sam, for short — who informed me that the Headmaster no less was extremely anxious to see me. Whereupon, having managed to fight off the effervescent Collins, I proceeded to the Head's study. Now, I wouldn't say that I've ever adopted an attitude of anything less than chronic subservience to the old sod, so I was mildly surprised and a little hurt to discover that I was to be reprimanded.

HELEN: What for?

JOHN: It seems that 5s — my form — are showing positive signs of anarchistic tendencies — long hair, smoking behind the toilets, usual sort of thing — and that the Headmaster along with a few other senior officials are putting it down to me.

HELEN: Do *you* smoke behind the toilets?

JOHN: Not when I should be at lessons, no. Anyway, to cut a short story long, it was impressed upon me that my liberal views and what he called my 'modern thinking' would have to be curbed.

HELEN: What was your reaction?

JOHN: I was hoping you'd ask. My reaction was carefully planned and, I thought, brilliantly executed. *(pause)* I said nothing.

HELEN: *(after a pause)* Was it a witty nothing or an insolent nothing?

JOHN: A bit of each, really. I stood, stared, scratched my head a few times and said nothing.

HELEN: With what effect?

JOHN: Well, after a few moments of listening to my silence the Headmaster coughed and said something which was obviously intended to remind me that I was now called upon to speak.

HELEN: And did you?

JOHN: No. I remained firm, resolute and silent. He then continued to prompt and suggest that I might have some opinion to cast on the matter and meanwhile waited for that opinion. Finally, he said that he wasn't prepared to argue with me and I was dismissed.

HELEN: From your job?

JOHN: From his study. If ever I won an argument with somebody who had no intention of having one, without saying a single word, it was today.

HELEN: *Have* you won?

JOHN: I don't doubt it. Throughout the rest of the day I received clandestine messages, and written notes from Sam, Collins that is, telling me that my name had been mentioned in such and such a place, or that the Head was greatly displeased, or that I was to be instantly sacked. All the signs.

HELEN: Of what?

JOHN: All the signs that I'd won. I'd flustered him. He'd never been confronted with such insubordinate tactics before and it genuinely shook him. He didn't know how to handle it. Anyway, later in the day I was summoned again. I went in and after a few words indicating that the morning's events were forgotten, the Headmaster said that he'd heard of a post in another school — better salary, more responsibility, etc. etc. — that might be of interest to me, and if so then a few words from him in the right places would as good as seal it.

HELEN: What? I take it you didn't repeat your earlier performance? Symbolic silence?

JOHN: No. I thanked him but said that I was quite happy where I was. What I didn't say was that the other school was far too far for me to travel, that more responsibility means less teaching, that I wasn't taking the bait and he wasn't getting rid of me that easily. *(pause)* That's what sort of day I've had.

HELEN: And in between the wheeling and dealing, did you find any time to spend in the classroom?

JOHN: Oh yes. Enough time, at any rate, for one of my fourth formers to ask me where babies come from, and for me to tell him with equal elegance that if he didn't know by now then he ought to bloody well find out without bothering me.

HELEN: Education's a wonderful thing.

JOHN: Well, I'm an English master not a biologist.

HELEN: Still, it wouldn't have hurt you to forget your syntax and your similes just once. You've always been rather blunt, you know?

JOHN: Well, he could have asked any one of the first formers. Aren't they the generation that everybody calls the 'rapid developers'? Anyway, it won't harm him to remain innocent for a few more years. Might save him from the odd infringement of the law.

HELEN: Knowledge isn't a crime. Although acquiring it from one's teacher apparently is. *(little pause)* You had a satisfactory day then?

JOHN: Above average. And you?

HELEN: Oh, by your standards I dare say it was uninviting. No reprimands, no jobs to turn down or pupils to swear at. I continued my humdrum course as usual without upset. And I got a letter from Jennifer.

JOHN: *(after a pause)* I thought you said there were no upsets?

HELEN: She's thinking of coming to stay for a few days. *(pause)* Well?

JOHN: Well what?

HELEN: Whatever it was that your Headmaster didn't do this morning to produce comment — let me know so that I can do it now.

JOHN: Meaning?

HELEN: Meaning Jennifer's thinking of coming to stay for a few days; what have you got against the idea?

JOHN: I've got nothing whatsoever against the idea, which in theory is perfectly sound. If your sister is thinking of coming to stay for a few days then that's fine by me just so long as she continues to think about it and not actually do it. Do you suppose it's an idle threat?

HELEN: No. So what have you got against it? You always have

something.

JOHN: Well then couldn't we just refer back to the last time we had this conversation and make my statement at that juncture suffice for this one?

HELEN: No, we couldn't.

JOHN: Why not?

HELEN: Because I've already written back and said it's okay.

JOHN: Oh dear, what a surprise.

HELEN: It's only for a few days.

JOHN: Yes, and we both know that a few days in Jennifer's case in fact means a week. At least; whenever she's not wanted she appears out of the blue and hangs on like the sword of Damocles, moralizing and sponging — which reminds me, she owes me ten pounds.

HELEN: She hasn't forgotten, but you can't expect her to repay you when you make it perfectly clear that she's not welcome.

JOHN: She could repay me by staying away. That would be ten pounds well spent. *(there is a ring at the* door) Don't tell me she's here already, she must have smelt the alcohol.

HELEN: *(rising to answer the door)* She won't get my letter until tomorrow. It's probably Peter, forgotten his key.
(Exits to the hall.)

JACK: *(off)* Hello, Helen. Is John home?

HELEN: *(off)* Hello, Jack. Yes, come in. *(JACK comes in followed by* HELEN*)*

JOHN: *(rising)* Hello, Jack, have you become nocturnal?

JACK: *(cold)* No. To tell you the truth, John, I've become wised up.

JOHN: Oh. Should I offer my congratulations, or perhaps just a drink? *(makes for the drinks trolley)*

JACK: Don't bother.

JOHN: Oh. Well, sit down anyway.

JACK: I'll stand.

JOHN: *(after a little pause)* Rather formal, aren't we?

JACK: I've not got much to say, only this: how long have we been friends?

JOHN: I don't know . . . . twenty-five years?

JACK: Twenty-six and a half years. I worked it out tonight while Angela was . . . . out. Does Helen know?

JOHN: That we've been friends for twenty-six and a half years?

HELEN: Does Helen know what, Jack?

JACK: *(to* HELEN*)* That you're married to a . . . . womanizer.

HELEN: I wasn't aware of it, no.

JACK: No. Nor was I.

JOHN: Well then that makes us all equal because I wasn't aware of it either. Would you mind telling me what you're talking about?

JACK: I think you know.

JOHN: I can assure you, Jack, I don't think I know any more than you do.

HELEN: Please, Jack, for my benefit at least, what's this about?

JACK: To be frank, Helen, your husband, my best friend, has been . . . . 'seeing' Angela, my wife, amongst others.

JOHN: I wasn't aware you had other wives, Jack.

HELEN: What do you mean, Jack?

JACK: I mean, Helen, and believe me I don't like having to say it, I mean that your husband is having an affair with my wife. *(A slight pause follows)*

HELEN: *(to* JOHN*)* Well?

JOHN: Well what?

HELEN: Have you been seeing Angela?

JOHN: Yes. Off and on, for twenty-six odd years. So have you.

HELEN: Don't be evasive, John.

JOHN: I wasn't being evasive.

HELEN: Being evasive has always been one of your talents.

JOHN: Really? A few moments ago I was informed that I'm always too blunt. Can one be evasively blunt?

HELEN: You haven't denied having an affair with Angela.

JOHN: Well, I've never denied that I played golf with Hitler but that's no reason to suppose that I did. *(pause)* Of course I'm not having an affair with Angela.

HELEN: How do you support this, Jack?

JACK: I'll tell you how. By Angela supposedly going to yoga classes on Thursday evenings — naturally, I didn't question it — by the odd phone call to your club, John — last Thursday evening — to find that you're not there; by another phone call that very same evening — thinking you might be here — to be told by Helen that you left the house saying you were going to that very same club; and by going to collect Angela from the P.T.A. meeting tonight and seeing the two of them together, walking in Princes Road obviously too enraptured by each other's company to notice me in the car watching them. Now that deals with Angela, but there is more, Helen, if you'd like to hear about the woman in the pub asking discreet questions about John's whereabouts. *(little pause)* Is that enough?

HELEN: *(after a pause)* That's quite an impressive list, John.

JOHN: As lists go.

HELEN: Do you deny any of it?

JOHN: No. Not the facts themselves anyway. Merely the intended implication.

HELEN: *(pouring herself a drink)* Then perhaps we'd better have some explanations?

JOHN: They, I'm afraid, are quite unimpressive. As explanations go. Where would you like to start?

HELEN: Well let's start with last Thursday, shall we? You said you were going to the club, when in fact Jack was told otherwise.

JOHN: Very well. Last Thursday, I left the house intending to go to the club as usual. However, I bumped into an old acquaintance en route who insisted on taking me to the Three Kings to let me buy him a drink. Several drinks in fact. I never got to the Club.

HELEN: Who was this acquaintance?

JOHN: I've really no idea.

HELEN: But if he was an acquaintance . . . .

JOHN: I had to take his word for that. All I know about him is that he likes drinking and talking, in that order.

HELEN: And tonight? Do you deny being with Angela?

JOHN: I don't deny it, but on reflection I do regret it. I went to the pub, as you are already aware, and met Angela, returning from her P.T.A. meeting, on the way home. We walked along together for some five minutes exchanging pleasantries until I turned off down here.

HELEN: You didn't tell me this.

JOHN: I didn't tell you this because when I got home you were in the middle of an uneventful bath. Since then it's slipped my mind, as events of no importance often do.

HELEN: What about the shady lady in the pub? Is she an old acquaintance?

JOHN: Not to my knowledge, but according to Jack she may shortly become a new one. *(There is a pause.)* No, Jack, I'm afraid you've got the wrong man.

HELEN: One of us certainly has.

JACK: You don't convince me, John. Not one iota.

JOHN: Good God, Jack, what about Angela? Surely you've tackled her?

JACK: Not yet.

JOHN: Well, Good God, do you honestly think she's the type that has affairs?

JACK: You're forgetting she had one once before.

JOHN: Well there you are then; she's had her fling. It was a disaster.

JACK: And you're trying to tell me that her single failure excludes the possibility of her trying again?

JOHN: No, I'm merely saying that she's already proved she's not very good at it, and if she was having another go you'd find out.

JACK: I have found out.

JOHN: *(losing patience)* Very well then, if your faith in Angela is such that you consider yoga classes and P.T.A. meetings to be mere alibis, then let's suppose that she is having an affair. But let's not suppose that she's having one with me because I don't go around seducing my best friend's wife.

JACK: You've yet to prove that.

JOHN: And you've yet to prove otherwise, so let's also not suppose that your lack of evidence is any stronger than my lack of evidence.

JACK: I suppose you want us all to be civilized about it, don't you? Polite? Rational?

JOHN: Yes, that doesn't sound like a bad idea considering the time.

JACK: The time? Considering the time? How about considering my marriage, eh?

JOHN: Believe me, Jack, I am considering your marriage, mine also, both of which may be a good deal less stable if we continue to argue the toss. Now why don't you go home, and I'm sure you'll find a very accommodating wife there waiting for you.

HELEN: That might not be a bad idea, Jack.

JACK: Yeh. *(Pause)* And you, Helen. You'll still be ' accommodating' with your husband tonight?

HELEN: That's for me to decide.

JACK: Yeh. Yes, it is.

JOHN: Well that's all sorted out then. Now why don't you run along home and sleep on it, or with it, whichever you prefer.

JACK: Yeh. Well, like I say, I'm wised up.

JOHN: Like you said. Your facts are rather distorted, your accusations somewhat mis-directed, and your verbosum lacking a certain panache, but other than that I suppose, yes, you're wised up.

JACK: *(after a pause)* Do you know what I think? I think that your type are rubbish. Compost on the otherwise clean face of the society. You deserve everything you get.

JOHN: Even your wife? Nobody deserves Angela like you do, she's very nearly undeserveable.

HELEN: *(quickly)* Hadn't we better stop this before we say things we don't mean?

JACK: It's a bit late for that, Helen.

JOHN: It's a bit late for most things, Jack, except going to bed.

JACK: Yes, that's your profession, isn't it? *(pause)* Anyway, don't expect miracles, Helen. I'm sorry it had to be done this way, but that's how it is. I'll see myself out. *(Exit. A pause follows, during which JOHN pours himself a drink.)*

JOHN: *(sitting down on sofa)* Well, that was all very entertaining, wasn't it?

HELEN: *(cold)* Was it?

JOHN: You didn't think so?

HELEN: Frankly, no.

JOHN: Admittedly, it was a bit pathetic, but old Jack does have a certain charm when he's excited.

HELEN: And what about you? Do you have a 'certain charm' when your best friend, who was obviously very upset comes here expecting a reasonable explanation and instead receives the full range of your sarcastic badinage?

JOHN: Darling, Jack gave up expecting reasonable explanations when Angela betrayed her vows with that architect chap. He came here tonight for a row, I wasn't prepared to give him one.

HELEN: You were very hostile towards him.

JOHN: I thought I was rather well restrained under the circumstances. What would you have done?

HELEN: *I* wouldn't have put myself in that position.

JOHN: And you think that I did?

HELEN: Jack obviously sees it that way.

JOHN: Jack isn't seeing it any way, only the way he wants to see it. In the morning he'll have calmed down.

HELEN: And then we can all forget it, is that the idea?

JOHN: I certainly shall.

HELEN: And what about these stories of yours? Bumping into old nameless friends, accidently meeting Angela, strange women in pubs . . . .

JOHN: They're hardly stories. Look, I've known Jack a long time. Tomorrow he'll be on the phone apologizing profusely, or he'll turn up here on the doorstep eating humble pie, and offering me a piece, which I shall accept in order to avoid the uncomfortable scene that I should have caused tonight. Then he'll rush off home to restore his marriage to the dubious standards to which it has grown accustomed. *(Pause. HELEN sits on armchair, left.)*

HELEN: While we restore ours?

JOHN: Meaning?

HELEN: Meaning even if Jack's accusations *are* the result of his imagination, perhaps his visit tonight has served a purpose. Enforced a sort of self-examination.

JOHN: Of what?

HELEN: Of us.

JOHN: You think we need it then?

HELEN: I'm merely suggesting the possibility.

JOHN: That we're heading for a crisis?

HELEN: If that's the word you want to use. It's all very easy to discard Jack's marriage as a failure, but what about ours?

JOHN: I didn't say that his marriage was a failure. I said Angela's affair was a failure which by comparison makes their marriage a relative success. Furthermore, I see nothing wrong with ours.

HELEN: It's not what you see; it's what you feel.

JOHN: I feel satisfied.

HELEN: Yes, but is that enough?

JOHN: Isn't it enough for you?

HELEN: I don't know, and that's the whole point. The time for re-assessment.

JOHN: And do you mean to say that this has all arisen from tonight's charade?

HELEN: No, I'm saying that it took tonight's incident to force the issue. Ignite it.

JOHN: *(after a pause)* You want to talk then?

HELEN: Yes.

JOHN: *(after a pause)* All right. We'll talk. *(There is a ring at the door.)*

HELEN: Saved by the bell. *(rises)* Must be Peter. *(Exits. Voices are heard in the hall. HELEN returns with PETER, a boy of about eighteen, and ADRIAN, a bit older, scruffy, long haired. ADRIAN's accent is obviously Northern.)*

PETER: Hello, dad. Forgot my key.

JOHN: So I see.

PETER: Mum, dad, this is Adrian. He's our Union President.

JOHN: Hello, Adrian.

ADRIAN: Hi.

HELEN: How did your meeting go?

PETER: Tremendous. Thanks to Adrian mainly. Isn't that right, Ade?

ADRIAN: Well . . . .

PETER: He's being modest. Mum, Ade's car has broken down, won't be able to fix it until the morning. Could we put him up for the night?

HELEN: Oh, well, yes. Yes, of course. I'll make the spare room up for him.

PETER: Great.

ADRIAN: Thanks, Mrs. Harding. Don't go to too much trouble.

HELEN: It's no trouble, really. *(to JOHN)* Entertain our guest while I fix the bed up.

JOHN: Right. *(HELEN exits)* What do you drink, Adrian?

ADRIAN: Thanks. I'll have a beer.

JOHN: Sorry, there's no beer at the moment. Er, gin, brandy, whisky, vodka, all the usual vices.

ADRIAN: Scotch then?

JOHN: Fine. Peter?

PETER: Yeh, the same. Thanks, dad.

    (JOHN pours the drinks.)

JOHN: There we are then. Do sit down.

ADRIAN: Thanks.

PETER: Thanks, dad. *(They sit:* JOHN *in his usual place on the sofa,* ADRIAN *in the armchair, left, and* PETER *on the sofa, the opposite end to* JOHN.*)*

JOHN: So. Your meeting was an eventual success then?

PETER: You bet. Thanks to Ade.

JOHN: And what do you propose to do about the threatened take-over?

PETER: Oh, there was all the usual talk, pseudo-revolutionary stuff — most of it rubbish.

JOHN: Such as?

PETER: Oh, suggestions of sit-ins, demos, non-attendance of lectures — timid, ineffective, well worn theories.

JOHN: How many turned up?

PETER: *(after a slight pause)* Six.

JOHN: Oh. Still, quality not quantity, eh? And it certainly seems to have been a lengthy meeting.

PETER: Oh, the meeting was over after half an hour.

JOHN: Oh?

PETER: Yes. We've been in the bar since eight.

JOHN: Ah, I see. Anyway, you're going to make a stand?

PETER: You bet. It was genius. Pure genius.

JOHN: Yes. *(Pause)* What was?

PETER: Ade's idea. There we all were, wasting time with . . . . chat, waiting for somebody to come up with something dynamic, and then Ade dropped the bombshell. You've got to hand it to him.

JOHN: What was the bombshell?

PETER: *(slight pause)* We're going to demolish the college.

JOHN: *(after a lengthy pause)* All of it?

PETER: As much as it takes to make our point. It's a protest, see.

JOHN: Yes. Well it's certainly not timid, let's hope it's not ineffective. But isn't that a little extreme?

ADRIAN: *(annoyed)* Extreme? It's an extreme situation, Mr. Harding. Do you realize that at the end of the year two hundred students will be leaving to go straight on the dole queue? It's the same all over the country — thousands of new qualifiers ending up as statistics on the unemployment list, or worse still in some office somewhere doing the work of a six year old. And what are the authorities doing about it? Providing jobs? No, they're going to turn the college over to the University, pretend we don't exist. That's giving up, isn't it? Conceding.

JOHN: Yes, but still . . . . how do you intend to set about this?

PETER: At night. Groups of us working in teams with chisels, hammers, anything we can lay our hands on, knocking away at the walls, brick by brick, taking the place apart — then they'll have to take notice.

JOHN: Surely you'll be heard?

ADRIAN: No. At night there's only the Bursar and a couple of old caretakers about, and even they'll go to bed eventually.

JOHN: But in the morning, surely, when the damage has been spotted —

ADRIAN: But what can they do? Seven hundred suspects, no clues to follow up — oh, there'll be police and uproar and panic of course, but the next night, or whenever the dust has settled we'll start again.

JOHN: And assuming you're at least partially successful — you think it will help you?

PETER: The University can't use a college that's in ruins, can it? There'll be nowhere to put them.

JOHN: But equally so with you surely?

ADRIAN: *(riled)* You don't like the idea then?

JOHN: On the contrary, I dare say it's very constructive in a destructive sort of way, but aren't you rather, as they say, cutting off your nose to spite your face? I mean, at this rate, by the time you've finished you'll all be eating, sleeping and taking lectures in one room, some of which I'm sure you're not used to.

PETER: It won't get that far, dad. We'll have won a long way before that. Anyway, it was a corporate decision and we're committed to it.

JOHN: But there were only six of you there.

ADRIAN: Makes no difference how many. We were representatives of our members and the vote was unanimous.

JOHN: You'll all end up in jail.

ADRIAN: You think so?

JOHN: Yes.

ADRIAN: Oh. Course, it's all right for you, isn't it?

JOHN: I beg your pardon?

ADRIAN: It's all right for you. You've never had to fight for your rights, have you? Never had to dirty your hands for a cause, eh?

JOHN: I don't think, Adrian, that you're fully qualified to speak —

ADRIAN: Ade.

JOHN: Sorry?

ADRIAN: I'm called Ade.

JOHN: Quite, and you're really not the best person to tell me what I've had to do in my life.

ADRIAN: No? Well I've heard all about you. Your bloody Head of Departmentship, your middle class values, your self satisfied, sardonic bloody airs —

JOHN: Remember, this is my house —

ADRIAN: Aye, how could I forget, eh? Couldn't be my bloody house, could it? I'm a student, aren't I? I've not got a job to go to, have I? When will I ever get a house, eh? Bloody never, that's when. Bloody never, so you can sneer and look down from your bloody high horse because it's easy, isn't it? Bloody easy to look down on people.

JOHN: I find it easy to look down on you, yes. *(HELEN returns.)*

HELEN: Right, the bed's all fixed.

JOHN: Adrian won't be stopping after all.

PETER: What?

JOHN: No, your friend is leaving, and next time you bring one home I suggest he has a wash prior to the event.

PETER: Dad!

JOHN: No arguments, please. Goodbye, Ade, I must say that meeting you has been a uniquely unpleasant and depressing experience. Peter will show you out.

ADRIAN: *(standing)* Right. Suits me. *(storms out.)*

PETER: Ade! *(Exits in pursuit. HELEN is still standing, bewildered, by the bookcase.)*

HELEN: What was all that about?

JOHN: Oh, nothing really. I was just ridding my house of six foot and twenty years of pollution. *(The front door slams. PETER returns.)*

PETER: I hope you're satisfied.

JOHN: You mean you hope I'm not.

PETER: Well, you should be. You always are. Self satisfied. Just like Ade said.

JOHN: Ade is a hooligan.

PETER: Ade is a great bloke. He's got guts, and I respect him. And that's more than I'll ever feel for you. *(Exits, slamming the door, pounding upstairs)*

HELEN: *(after a pause)* Well?

JOHN: Well what?

HELEN: Aren't you going upstairs?

JOHN: What for?

HELEN: To apologize to him.

JOHN: For what?

HELEN: You made him look small. How do you expect him to face his friends when they discover his father is a bigot?

JOHN: I suspect they know that already. Peter seems to keep them well informed. *(pause)* If Adrian is an example of the intellectual set that we're always hearing so much about, then this country's finished.

HELEN: You could have been a little more tolerant.

JOHN: They're planning to knock down the college. Peter kept telling me about this brilliant scheme to protest with, and that was it. Adrian's idea, and our son calls him a genius.

HELEN: They're trying to save their futures.

JOHN: Adrian's future seems fairly well mapped out for him, to be spent mainly behind bars I should think, the sooner the better. *(JOHN pours himself another drink, and returns to the sofa. HELEN sits on the armchair, left.)*

HELEN: We were going to talk.

JOHN: Were we?

HELEN: Yes.

JOHN: I think I've had enough talking for tonight.

HELEN: But not enough drinking?

JOHN: No. So why don't you go and console the prodigal son, and I'll get quietly drunk?

HELEN: And what about . . . . things?

JOHN: Things? Things will continue in much the same vein as usual I expect. They generally do.

HELEN: Until the next time?

JOHN: Until the next time, what?

HELEN: Until the next time we have this conversation.

JOHN: We're not having a conversation. At least I'm not.

HELEN: Don't you care anymore?

JOHN: I fail to see where all this is leading. You want to talk, I don't. Peter and his cronies want to knock down colleges. I don't. Jack wants to believe his wife is having an affair. I don't. You want your sister to come and stay for a few decades. I don't. I mean, what's the point? Until this evening we had continued along our merry course, quite happily I'd assumed, uncatastrophic apart from the odd trauma and marital tiff, and then because of one evening of uninterrupted interruptions, accusations and insults from assorted friends and relations, we have to sit down and start having conversations, and get the notebooks out for re-assessments and examinations. *(pause)* Don't I care about what anymore?

HELEN: *(after a pause)* Anything.

(A slight pause. JOHN looks at HELEN, then:)

BLACKOUT and CURTAIN

ACT II
Scene 1

Friday afternoon, the room is empty and a little untidy.
JOHN enters from the kitchen, rolling down his sleeves, and
pours himself a drink. It should be implied that he has already
had several drinks, but he isn't drunk. He sits on the sofa and
picks up the newspaper. While he is reading, JENNIFER
enters silently from the hall, wearing an overcoat and holding
a small suitcase.

JENNIFER: Hello, John.

JOHN: *(looking round)* Oh. How did you get in?

JENNIFER: I have a key, remember?

JOHN: Ah. Well, I haven't got a case for breaking and entering
then. But you've got yours, I see. *(little pause)* Case, I mean.
(pause) Anyway, sit down, sister-in-law, or can't you stop?

JENNIFER: *(removing her coat)* Do you always have to be so
unpleasant?

JOHN: No. I don't have to; I do it out of the goodness of my
heart.

JENNIFER: *(puts her coat over the armchair, left, and sits)* I
didn't expect to find you here.

JOHN: Sorry. *(pause)* Where did you expect to find me?

JENNIFER: What I meant was, I thought you'd be at school.
Why aren't you?

JOHN: I'm taking a long deserved rest. How about you?

JENNIFER: Oh, I'm between jobs.

JOHN: What happened to the export business?

JENNIFER: We didn't get on.

JOHN: Oh? When did you decide that?

JENNIFER: About three weeks ago.

JOHN: Oh. You hadn't been there long had you? When did you start exactly?

JENNIFER: Four weeks ago. Actually, it was the export business that decided we didn't get on.

JOHN: Ah. *(obviously not interested)*

JENNIFER: How's Peter?

JOHN: Oh, on the occasions that we've passed comment to each other over the last few days he seemed in fine spirits.

JENNIFER: Is he enjoying college?

JOHN: Distinctly. Lectures and studying appear to be optional extras, whilst the little time that he doesn't spend cavorting in the gymnasium he spends plotting to get rid of it.

JENNIFER: I don't follow.

JOHN: No, well don't worry because I don't either. *(pause)* You've got your suitcase.

JENNIFER: So you've said. Was it an observation or a question?

JOHN: Oh, not a question as such. But I might enquire why.

JENNIFER: Why?

JOHN: Why you have your suitcase, I mean. Not why is it a suitcase, or anything quite so Freudian as that, but why you have a suitcase at all, assuming that it's full of overnight things like the average one?

JENNIFER: Helen got my letter.

JOHN: Is that a question?

JENNIFER: No. I wrote to Helen and she invited me to come and stay for a few days.

JOHN: (after a pause) Am I to understand that in the letter you wrote to Helen, she invited you to come and stay?

JENNIFER: You're being deliberately stupid. She wrote back to me and said I was welcome to come and stay in her letter.

JOHN: Helen said you were welcome to come and stay in her letter? Oh, you mean, in her letter, Helen said you were welcome to come and stay. She didn't tell you we don't have any spare money

JENNIFER: I didn't ask.

JOHN: Well that doesn't usually stop us from having to tell you.

JENNIFER: Where *is* Helen? Isn't Friday her afternoon off?

JOHN: Yes.

JENNIFER: Can't you be more specific?

JOHN: How do you mean?

JENNIFER: I mean, do you know where she is. If so, when she will be back?

JOHN: In answer to your first question – no, consequently, in answer to your second – I've no idea.

JENNIFER: Have you given up communicating?

JOHN: No, only talking.

JENNIFER: I can see that. *(facetiously)* Is she leaving you?

JOHN: No. Or to be more specific, yes. Past tense though.

JENNIFER: *(somewhat taken aback)* Oh. When did this happen?

JOHN: Yesterday. You're the first to know, from the family, I mean. Peter has been at friends since yesterday, so as far as I know he's not aware yet. *(a slight pause follows)*

JENNIFER: *(getting up)* Can I have a drink? I'd given up hoping you might offer me one.

JOHN: I don't usually have to offer. I've grown accustomed to just throwing away the empty bottles. (JENNIFER *pours herself a drink)*

JENNIFER: There's no one else is there? *(sits)*

JOHN: Good God, no. You don't think Helen's the type to run off with the milkman, do you?

JENNIFER: *(after a pause)* She should have done it years ago.

JOHN: No, our milkman's a remarkably boring sort of chap, even by Helen's standards, and he's got an artificial leg.

JENNIFER: *(ignoring his flippancy)* So how did it happen?

JOHN: Doodlebug, I believe.

JENNIFER: John, please. I'm trying to be helpful.

JOHN: Oh, I see. And when you said that Helen should have left me years ago, that was your idea of being helpful, was it?

JENNIFER: I'm sorry. *(pause)* Do you want to talk about it?

JOHN: No, but as you do, I haven't much choice, have I?

JENNIFER: What made her go?

JOHN: Oh, Helen's easily provoked. I'm having an affair.

JENNIFER: *(after a pause)* You surprise me, John. Who with?

JOHN: My best friend's wife. Assuming, of course, that he *is* still my best friend, and she is still his wife.

JENNIFER: How long has it been going on?

JOHN: Since Wednesday, I believe. At least, that's when I was first told about it.

JENNIFER: I'm not playing games with you, John. What do you mean?

JOHN: I mean this: that on Wednesday night, Jack Brandon came around here, called me a few names, accused me of being his wife's lover and generally made my life hell; consequently, Peter's friend Adrian insulted me, Peter followed suit, and Helen came over all philosophical, by which time her suspicions were sufficiently aroused for her to pack up and take flight when, as I am told in the note that Helen left for me yesterday, an unknown woman called here asking for me. That's as much as I know.

JENNIFER: You mean this business of you having an affair is a joke?

JOHN: Well, nobody's laughed much as yet.

JENNIFER: And Helen's taken it seriously?

JOHN: Apparently. *(The front door closes, and* PETER *enters.)*

PETER: *(to* JENNIFER*)* Hello. How are you?

JENNIFER: Very well, thank you, Peter. And you?

PETER: Okay. Are you staying for a while?

JENNIFER: I might do.

PETER: *(making an effort to be polite)* Great. *(to* JOHN*)* Where's mum?

JOHN: Um, your mother's gone away for a few days.

PETER: Where?

JOHN: Oh . . . . those people, her friends . . . . Andy and . . . . his wife.

PETER: Andy and Rachel?

JOHN: Exactly. Yes. Andy and Rachel.

PETER: Why?

JOHN: Well, I don't know. To see them, I suppose.

PETER: Oh. *(pause)* Why aren't you at school?

JOHN: I didn't feel like school. Why aren't you at college? Assuming it's still standing, of course.

PETER: I didn't feel like it.

JOHN: Ah. How's the demolition going?

PETER: It's not.

JOHN: Oh dear, why not?

PETER: Ade. He backed out.

JOHN: But, Good God, it was his idea, wasn't it?

PETER: Yeh. Well, he backed out.

JOHN: But what about the others?

PETER: Some of them backed out as well.

JOHN: How many.

PETER: All of them. Except me and George.

JOHN: Oh. Well, at least George stuck to his guns then. Is he good with a chisel?

PETER: George is a girl. *(pause)* When will mum be back?

JOHN: Er . . . when Rosemary's better.

PETER: Rachel.

JOHN: What?

PETER: Andy's wife is Rachel, not Rosemary.

JOHN: Ah. When Rachel's better.

PETER: What's wrong with her?

JOHN: Um, that disease . . . mexymatosis, I think.

PETER: She can't have that. Only animals get that.

JOHN: Ah. Well, perhaps she caught it off her daughter then. *(PETER moves to the telephone and looks at the pad of numbers)* Who are you phoning?

PETER: Mum.

JOHN: Why?

PETER: Because I want to speak to her.

JOHN: I'll give her a message if you like?

PETER: But you don't know when she's coming back, do you? *(starts to dial)*

JOHN: Actually I wouldn't bother.

PETER: Why not?

JOHN: She's not there.

PETER: *(replacing the receiver)* Where is she then?

JOHN: I don't know.

PETER: *(coming round the front of the sofa)* And Rachel's not ill?

JOHN: Well, she certainly hasn't got mexymatosis according to you.

PETER: Then why the fiction?

JOHN: The fact is, Peter, your mother has gone away for a few days to think things over.

PETER: What things?

JOHN: In general.

PETER: Like a separation then?

JOHN: Very similar, yes.

PETER: Good for her. *(little pause)* I'm going out for a while.
     Might be back tonight, I might not.

JOHN: Fine. *(PETER moves towards the door.)* Peter.

PETER: *(turning)* What?

JOHN: Maybe we can have a talk some time?

PETER: Maybe. *(to* JENNIFER*)* Bye.

JENNIFER: Goodbye, Peter. *(PETER leaves. A slight pause
     follows)* You handled that well, didn't you?

JOHN: I never answer rhetorical questions.

JENNIFER: You've upset him.

JOHN: I don't believe today's youth get upset about anything.
     Most things they're indifferent to.

JENNIFER: Why are you on such dodgy ground with each other?

JOHN: We had a tiff about student Union policy, following which
     I threw his friend out of the house, following which he hasn't
     spoken to me, except in telegramic prose.

JENNIFER: Not been your week, has it?

JOHN: I never answer —

JENNIFER: — rhetorical questions, yes, you said. *(pause)* So.
     Going back to your original problem — perhaps we could
     have a recap. Helen has packed her bags and gone, firstly
     because she believes that you are having or have had an affair
     with your friend Jack's wife, secondly because of a suspicious
     visit from a strange woman whose identity you're presumably
     unaware of, with a possible third reason being that you've
     failed not only as a husband but as a father as well. Is that the
     gist of it?

JOHN: Barring minor details.

JENNIFER: Such as?

JOHN: Such as, I don't for a minute believe that Helen believes
     I'm having an affair. In fact, she knows I'm not; I've already
     explained to her the geographical impossibility of such a thing
     occurring. Furthermore, I'm not yet guilty of failing as a
     father, although I'm working on it, and the only reason that
     Helen has departed is *because* I'm not guilty of that and the

other assorted slanders, rather than in spite of it. *(pause)* She'll be back.

JENNIFER: You think so? And what about the unknown lady caller?

JOHN: She will hopefully remain unknown.

JENNIFER: *(after a pause)* How did Jack get these ideas about you and his wife?

JOHN: *(rising to get a drink)* He has a fertile imagination and a flirtatious wife, both of which run away from time to time.

JENNIFER: You don't seem to be unduly concerned about all this.

JOHN: Should I be?

JENNIFER: Well, aren't you, as they say, going through a crisis?

JOHN: Helen's going through a crisis; I'm going through a bottle of Scotch. *(sits)* God, I've played my part as the ever loving husband for twenty years. Remembered our anniversary religiously, brought her breakfast in bed annually, mended the fuses, paid the bills . . . . and what have I got to show for all this devotion? My best friend hates me, my wife's left me, my son resents me . . . . I should be the one to leave.

JENNIFER: *(after a pause)* Have you any idea where Helen might be?

JOHN: Not the slightest.

JENNIFER: Have you phoned my mother?

JOHN: Not since nineteen sixty three, why?

JENNIFER: It might be worth a try. I'll ring her if you like.

JOHN: No, thanks. I'd have to sell the house to pay the telephone bill.

JENNIFER: To my way of thinking, John, I'm wasting my sympathy on you.

JOHN: I wasn't aware you had a way of thinking. Anyway, as you've already said that Helen should have done this years ago, there would seem to be a shadow of a doubt on your sincerity.

JENNIFER: Sympathy and sincerity are two different things, John, and I have a certain amount of both.

JOHN: I would have said you have a certain amount of neither. *(The front door bell rings.)* Be a good girl and answer that for me. *(A slight pause. Then JENNIFER gets up and goes into the hall.)*

COLLINS: *(off)* Hello, is Mr. Harding at home?

JENNIFER: *(off)* Yes. Come in. *(JENNIFER returns, ushering COLLINS into the room.)*

JOHN: Well, well, Sam, this is a surprise. Sit down.

COLLINS: Thank you. *(sits in armchair, left)*

JOHN: Jennifer, this is our Social Activities Master, Sam for short. Sam, this is Jennifer.

COLLINS: Pleased to meet you.

JENNIFER: Hello.

JOHN: *(rising)* Perhaps I can get you a drink?

COLLINS: No, thanks, old boy. Only drink under stress.

JOHN: Oh. Well, perhaps, in that case, you won't mind if I have one?

COLLINS: No, no, please. *(JOHN pours himself a drink.)*

JENNIFER: Well, if you gentlemen will excuse me, I'll take my things upstairs. *(COLLINS stands as JOHN sits.)*

COLLINS: Very nice meeting you.

JENNIFER: Thank you. *(exit)*

COLLINS: Charming woman.

JOHN: *(after a pause; impassive)* Where?

COLLINS: Your wife, I meant.

JOHN: Oh. Oh, yes. Thank you. What about my sister-in-law?

COLLINS: *(puzzled)* Sorry?

JOHN: What is your considered opinion of my sister-in-law?

COLLINS: Well . . . . I don't believe I've met her.

JOHN: You just did, but don't worry because I didn't believe it at first either.

COLLINS: Oh? So that wasn't your wife then?

JOHN: No, my wife isn't here at the moment. You just missed her by a day or two.

COLLINS: Oh.

JOHN: *(after a little pause)* Are you sure I can't offer you a drink?

COLLINS: No, no, really. I've got *(tapping his briefcase)* a thousand timetables to work on tonight.

JOHN: *(clearly not seeing any relevance at all)* Oh, I see.

COLLINS: No, I just called to see . . . . well actually, Headmaster asked me to drop in on my way home to see if you were O.K.

JOHN: Well, that's very decent of him. And of you, of course.

Actually, I'm fine.

COLLINS: Oh, good. It was just that, well, with you not being in today, and, well, er, what with your little tete a tete with Headmaster the other day . . . .

JOHN: Sorry? *(as if not remembering)*

COLLINS: Um, your talk with the Headmaster about . . . .

JOHN: Oh, that! Good God, I'd forgotten completely about that. Oh and you think that our conversation on, let me see, Wednesday, had something to do with my not being in today?

COLLINS: Well . . . .

JOHN: Good God, no. Believe me, there are no grudges borne on my side at least. It was merely a misunderstanding. No hard feelings. In fact, the Headmaster went to great pains on my behalf to find another job for me.

COLLINS: Yes, I heard.

JOHN: Not my sphere, of course, but a kind thought. Why don't you go for it?

COLLINS: Sorry?

JOHN: This other job.

COLLINS: Oh. Well, of course, it's not my sphere either, really. I mean . . . .

JOHN: Of course, and then also, perhaps Headmaster hasn't suggested it to you?

COLLINS: Well, no, but . . . . besides . . . .

JOHN: Yes?

COLLINS: Well *(furtively)* I was perhaps hoping for higher things.

JOHN: *(after a little pause)* Good God, you're not running for Captain of the Bridge Team, are you?

COLLINS: No. Actually, there have been rumours, purely rumours mind you, about Mr. Ainsworth . . . .

JOHN: Of course! He must be ninety if he's a day. Ah, I see the way your mind is working.

COLLINS: *(warming to the conversation and lowering his voice, furtively)* Yes. You see, the story goes that Mr. Ainsworth is retiring at the end of term, and that leaves the way clear, so to speak, for applications for Deputy Head.

JOHN: Yes, I see it all now. If you can get that Deputy Head's job, then, Good God, within a year or two, it's a clear run to captaincy of the Bridge Team. I congratulate you, Sam.

COLLINS: Anyway, I don't want to speak prematurely, but . . . .

other rumours have it that should Mr. Ainsworth step down, then I'm, shall we say, in with a chance.

JOHN: Oh? Strange.

COLLINS: *(a pause)* How do you mean?

JOHN: Oh, nothing really.

COLLINS: Please, if you've heard anything . . . .

JOHN: Oh, gossip, merely. *(*COLLINS *waits in expectation)* Well, it was just that I've heard rumours, as you put it, that old Cartwright is a dead cert for Ainsworth's job.

COLLINS: What? Cartwright? I can't imagine anything more remote. Where did you hear this?

JOHN: Oh, it was just something that slipped out during my chat with the Headmaster the other day.

COLLINS: *(deflated)* He told you!

JOHN: Well . . . . *(gestures)*

COLLINS: Well I . . . . *(utterly flabbergasted)*

JOHN: Shouldn't pay too much attention to it, Sam — gossip, that's all.

COLLINS: But if the Headmaster said —

JOHN: Exactly. Worst gossip in the school.

COLLINS: Well . . . . *(recovers his composure slowly)* Anyway, I just called to see if you were all right.

JOHN: Well, I'm fine, Sam. As a matter of fact, I've been taking things easy.

COLLINS: Yes. *(pause)* Naturally, we were a bit stuck at first, what with the already acute staff shortage, but Headmaster and I put our heads together and got round it all right.

JOHN: My trust in you was well placed then.

COLLINS: Yes. Er, Mr. Jarvis kindly stepped in for your English and Miss Inglewood swapped with Mr. Hughes for the biology practical.

JOHN: Good God, she must have been exhausted.

COLLINS: *(uncomfortable)* Er, what I meant was, Mr. Hughes did the biology, while Miss Inglewood covered your afternoon periods.

JOHN: Oh, of course. *(pause)* Do you know what my form call Miss Inglewood?

COLLINS: No.

JOHN: Nicholas.

COLLINS: Nicholas?

JOHN: Yes. Derived from knicker-less. Apparently they heard a story that one night after a staff party she went home without her knickers.

COLLINS: What? Who on earth told them such an outrageous lie?

JOHN: I believe I did.

COLLINS: What?

JOHN: Yes. And do you know what my form call you?

COLLINS: Me?

JOHN: Creepy. Creepy Collins, derived from the fact that you crawl to the Headmaster. Up his ass, as they put it.

COLLINS: *(genuinely indignant)* From information supplied by you, no doubt?

JOHN: Yes, I believe I have contributed the odd ancedote now and again. The latest news should go down rather well, don't you think? That Creepy Collins has possibly creeped for the last time, as even creepier Cartwright seems all set for the Deputy Headship.

COLLINS: *(rising)* I really don't think I've got the time —

JOHN: No, Collins, neither have I, so why don't you run along home and play with your timetables and unleash all that pent up nervous energy on Mrs. Collins, better still ring up the Headmaster and demand to know exactly how long one has to suck up to the old bugger before such devotion is rewarded. Now why don't you do that?

COLLINS: Yes, but —

JOHN: *(rising as JENNIFER returns)* Now don't worry your head with questions, trot along like a good boy and don't talk to any strangers. *(JENNIFER watches as JOHN ushers COLLINS out into the hall.)* Goodbye, then, old sport, give Headmaster a kiss for me. *(Front door closes)*

JENNIFER: *(as JOHN returns)* Did he really deserve that?

JOHN: Probably not, but I'm not asking any favours in return. *(sits)* So what are you going to do?

JENNIFER: *(sitting)* How do you mean?

JOHN: Well, I take it you haven't come to visit me?

JENNIFER: Is that a gentle reminder that I'm not welcome?

JOHN: It wasn't meant to be. Gentle, I mean.

JENNIFER: I see. *(pause. She rises and moves to the telephone)*

JOHN: What are you doing?

JENNIFER: Phoning my mother.

JOHN: You're wasting your time.

JENNIFER: *(dialling)* I've been doing that since I arrived. *(pause, then, speaking into the receiver)* Hello, mother, it's Jennifer . . . . How are you? . . . . Good, yes I'm fine . . . . Listen, mother, is Helen with you? . . . . Oh, no, it's just that I can't get a reply at her home . . . . no, nothing important . . . . yes, I see, mother . . . . Anyway, I can't stop, I'll try again later . . . . O.K. . . . . Yes, mother . . . . Fine . . . . Goodbye. *(replaces receiver)* She's not there.

JOHN: Well, I hate to say I told you so.

JENNIFER: *(sitting)* Aren't you worried at all?

JOHN: Helen will be back when she's had time to think things over.

JENNIFER: You hope.

JOHN: You're sure this is leading to something, aren't you?

JENNIFER: Let's just say I'm optimistic. *(pause)* What did she take with her?

JOHN: Oh, a few clothes. The customary toothbrush, of course, make-up, probably about three trunkfuls, and a bit of money she had hidden, but not very well hidden.

JENNIFER: Is that all? Has she left anything important?

JOHN: Like an iron lung, you mean? What's important to the average wife on the run? Mascara? Deodorant? Or perhaps the ten gallon jar of cottonwool balls? Her dressing table actually resembles a dressing table again instead of a chemist shop, having in former years been smothered in lotions, potions and pills, both medicinal and cosmetic . . . . But the sun-ray lamp is still gathering dust on top of the wardrobe; that might be a clue although I warn you that it hasn't done much else for the last three summers.

JENNIFER: Well, I can't see her returning to the matrimonial home for the sake of a sun-ray lamp.

JOHN: Well, if you were leaving your husband, assuming, of course, that you had one, and assuming also that you left him before he left you, what would you take with you, apart from the gin?

JENNIFER: I would leave nothing except the bills and the washing up.

JOHN: Then your absence would have much the same effect as

your presence, I imagine. *(little pause)* No, I really don't know what Helen's likely to need that she hasn't already taken. Unless, of course, she plans a permanent departure, in which case I suppose even the sun lamp will become something of a nomad.

JENNIFER: I'd like another drink if that's all right. *(rises to go to the trolley)* Suppose this is more serious than you think?

JOHN: Which? Your drinking or my marriage?

JENNIFER: Your marriage; the lack of it. *(sitting)*

JOHN: You don't believe in marriage, do you?

JENNIFER: Only at the right time and to the right person.

JOHN: And you'd know about these things, wouldn't you? Being my favourite spinster-in-law?

JENNIFER: I know that your only hope is that Helen isn't impressed with these stories about you.

JOHN: Oh, I don't think she was impressed. *(pause)*

JENNIFER: When do you intend going back to school?

JOHN: Oh . . . . Monday . . . . Tuesday . . . . Wednesday, that sort of thing.

JENNIFER: And what will be their attitude towards your absence?

JOHN: Absence makes the heart grow fonder and the school terms grow shorter . . . . they can take any attitude they wish to. The English Department can't function without me, so I don't expect drastic measures.

JENNIFER: You consider yourself indispensable?

JOHN: Only to those things to which I make myself indispensable. But is this third degree really necessary? I mean, you've made your point, had your fun and O.K. stay the night if it'll make you feel any happier, but must I be put through this interrogation? If I decide that I'm in need of pointless questions then I'll go back to school and get paid for answering them.

JENNIFER: I'm glad you can joke about it.

JOHN: Does the situation call for two minutes silence then? I thought you'd enjoy a good laugh at my expense.

JENNIFER: Oh, I shall laugh, John. This time next week or next month or whatever . . . . I'll laugh so loudly that you'll hear me when you're here alone, smoking in bed till all hours, wondering where she is, who she's with, rushing down to the mat in the morning to find the letter that's not there, until at last you drown yourself in whisky and then probably the Thames . . . . that's when I'll laugh, John. Perhaps you'll laugh with me?

JOHN: *(after a pause)* As a matter of fact, I never smoke in bed as Helen would testify on the odd occasions when she's been awake to see me not smoking. The thing is, you see, I don't really care about your opinions for what they're worth, which isn't much. The thing is that Helen probably doesn't care either. You see, as a sister you've been a pretty bad second best. Every time you come here it's at your own invitation, and when you leave it's only because our hints have become so blatent that a slab of rock would have difficulty misunderstanding them. I find your company uniquely uninspiring and your capacity for other people's alcohol is remarkable by any standards, on top of which you have never been content with merely haunting us on the telephone, but insist on these personal visits to prove that you actually are as dislikeable as I've always said you were — and it's only because you happen to be Helen's sister that you are still here now, drinking my gin and breathing my air. *(Pause. JENNIFER is obviously crushed by this outburst. However, she recovers a little of her composure.)*

JENNIFER: Must we go on like this? At each other's throats for twenty years? Can't we make it easier for ourselves?

JOHN: Oh, I agree entirely. It's only because I'm married to your sister that we bother to insult each other at all. If it wasn't for that I would hope we wouldn't even speak.

JENNIFER: *(after a pause)* You are a hateful bastard.

JOHN: Yes, that's what my fourth form tell me.

JENNIFER: *(slight pause; she is still trying to keep some of her dignity)* I'll go tomorrow morning.

JOHN: Yes, well don't rush off; first light of day will suffice. *(pause)* Do you know, I'd quite forgotten that I haven't eaten a thing all day? I think there's a packet of tinned soup, or perhaps I could warm up a salad for us?

JENNIFER: I'll fix something if you like.

JOHN: Splendid. A hint accepted is a hint not wasted.

JENNIFER: *(rising)* Do you mind if I have a shower first?

JOHN: By my guest, figuratively speaking.

JENNIFER: Right. *(she turns towards the door, hesitates)* Do you know something? I don't believe you could ever understand me. Not in a million years.

JOHN: *(after a pause)* Then I have something to be grateful for after all. *(Slight pause, then JENNIFER leaves, shutting the door behind her. JOHN remains seated. Slight pause, then:)*

CURTAIN

ACT II
Scene 2

The stage is empty, and there is a ring at the door followed shortly by voices in the hall. Then, JENNIFER enters ushering AMANDA and FRANK into the room.

JENNIFER: If you wouldn't mind waiting in here, I'll give him a shout.

AMANDA: Thank you. *(JENNIFER exits to hall leaving the door open.)*

JENNIFER: John. It's for you.

JOHN: *(off)* Just coming. *(JENNIFER returns)*

JENNIFER: He won't be a moment. Won't you sit down?

AMANDA: Thank you. *(they sit on the sofa)*

JENNIFER: You're friends of John?

AMANDA: Well, I am. An old friend.

JENNIFER: Oh, I see. I'm John's sister-in-law, Jennifer.

AMANDA: Very pleased to meet you. Amanda Robertson. Formerly Thorpe. And this is my husband Frank, formerly a wiser man than he is now.

FRANK: How do you do?

JENNIFER: Hello. *(JOHN enters)* Oh, some friends of yours, John. *(AMANDA and FRANK stand.)*

JOHN: Really? *(pause)* Have we met?

AMANDA: You don't recognize me then?

JOHN: No. *(pause)* Sorry, should I?

AMANDA: I should hope so after all those times we had together in Copley Wood.

JOHN: *(after a pause)* I really can't remember the three of us ever having been in or even near Copley Wood. Was I sober at the time?

AMANDA: Oh, quite sober. And there was only the two of us.

JOHN: Oh, good. *(pause)* Sorry, I really — *(sudden recognition)* Good God! Amanda!

AMANDA: Long time no see.

JOHN: Well, it must be, let me see, over twenty years?

AMANDA: Is it really that long? Anyway. John, this is my husband Frank. Frank this is John Harding.

FRANK: *(shaking hands)* Pleased to meet you.

JOHN: Hello. I must say this is a surprise. *(clearly not at all pleased to see them)* What are you doing in this neck of the woods?

AMANDA: Looking for you, of course.

JOHN: Oh. *(slight pause)* Why?

AMANDA: Oh, I saw your name at the end of a letter in the Times Ed. and I thought 'could that be the same John Harding that I used to know?'

JOHN: Oh, so somebody read it then?

AMANDA: Yes. Very impressive. You treated your subject with great . . . . magnanimity, shall we say?

JOHN: Thank you. *(pause)* What *was* the subject?

AMANDA: Why, the Crompton Report, of course. Had you forgotten?

JOHN: I was trying to.

AMANDA: Oh. *(pause)* Married now, I see?

JOHN: Yes. *(pause)* Oh, this isn't my wife. *(referring to JENNIFER)* This is my sister-in-law, Jennifer.

AMANDA: I know.

JOHN: You know?

AMANDA: Of course. Does your wife know about us?

JOHN: Us?

AMANDA: That we had, you know, a thing going?

JOHN: Good God, that was years before I even met Helen.

AMANDA: Yes, still you know how wives are.

JOHN: Ah. Er, you said you knew that Jennifer wasn't my wife?

AMANDA: Yes, she told me before you came down.

JOHN: Oh.

AMANDA: And, of course, I met your wife the other day.

Didn't she tell you?

JOHN: No. Unless . . . . it was you who called yesterday?

AMANDA: That's right. She didn't mind, did she?

JOHN: Good God, no. *(pause)* Perhaps you'd like a drink?

AMANDA: I'd love one. Gin and orange, please.

JOHN: Fine. Frank?

FRANK: Cheers. Scotch, please. *(JOHN pours drinks)*

JENNIFER: Before you offer me one, John, I'm going out.

JOHN: Well, if you're sure.

JENNIFER: Goodbye, Amanda, Frank.

AMANDA: Goodbye.

FRANK: Cheerio. *(JENNIFER exits)*

AMANDA: *(taking drink from JOHN)* Your wife didn't say anything then, John?

JOHN: When?

AMANDA: About my little visit? She didn't mind?

JOHN: She didn't say so in so many words, no.

AMANDA: But her tone, surely? Must have given you an idea.

JOHN: My wife's handwriting displays no particular tone. I haven't seen Helen since yesterday morning.

AMANDA: Oh, she's away then?

JOHN: Very much so, yes.

AMANDA: Oh. It's just that she seemed a little − you know.

JOHN: I daresay.

AMANDA: Everything's all right then?

JOHN: Good God, yes.

AMANDA: Only she did seem a little −

JOHN: How my wife seemed, whether in little or large quantities has nothing whatsoever to do with things being all right, or not, as the case may be. *(pause)* This is just a social call then?

AMANDA: Oh, yes. I couldn't resist the opportunity of seeing how you'd fared since those days in Copley Wood. The last time I heard from you, you stood me up.

JOHN: *(after a pause)* If I stood you up, how did you hear from me?

AMANDA: Oh, I didn't. Not afterwards, anyway. We arranged a meeting place and you didn't show up.

JOHN: Oh? Well, I'm sure there was a perfectly sound reason for it if I did fail to show, which quite honestly I don't remember, and even if I did I'm sure Frank wouldn't want to be bored with hearing all about it, so let's change the subject? You got my address from the school I take it?

AMANDA: Yes, although not at first. I hunted about in the area for a while, pubs, etc. then when that didn't prove forthcoming I rang them back and asked. Should have done that in the first place.

JOHN: So that's another mystery solved.

AMANDA: Sorry?

JOHN: It's just that I'd heard rumours of a certain party asking after me — as it turns out, you're that certain party.

AMANDA: I see. Must have sounded suspicious.

JOHN: Vaguely.

AMANDA: Yes. *(pause)* I'd always wondered what had become of you since that last time we didn't meet.

JOHN: Well, this is it. House, wife, family, all the usual symptoms.

AMANDA: Symptoms? Of what?

JOHN: Oh, that in twenty years you haven't missed much. And there's Frank, of course, who has been, I'm sure, a more than adequate substitute.

AMANDA: Oh, yes. Still, my curiosity is satisfied at least.

JOHN: Well that's all right then.

AMANDA: You know, that last time — when you didn't show up — I really thought that something had happened to you.

JOHN: Well, I'm sorry I can't offer that excuse. I expect it was some trifling thing; the war, perhaps, or my graduation into long trousers.

AMANDA: Oh, now, come on, John. We're not talking about a couple of love struck children. This was nineteen fifty something.

JOHN: Was it really? *(pause)* Perhaps I can offer you a cigarette? *(pulls a packet from his jacket pocket)*

AMANDA: Thank you.

FRANK: No, thanks, old boy.

AMANDA: Frank doesn't believe in it. Says it's a health hazard. He expects to outlive me.

JOHN: Oh? Well, good luck, Frank.

FRANK: Thanks.

AMANDA: Actually he used to smoke. In fact Frank and I met whilst buying a packet of cigarettes.

JOHN: Not the same packet, presumably? *(pause)* What do you do, Frank? For a living.

FRANK: I'm in housing. Telling people that a railway line is going to run through their front room, that sort of thing.

JOHN: Satisfying work then?

FRANK: I find it so, yes.

JOHN: I can well imagine. That's the trouble with teaching nowadays. It's not ruthless enough.

FRANK: Really?

JOHN: Yes. We only had one case of cruelty last year. The magistrate had an uneasy time.

AMANDA: So the child's parents sued, did they?

JOHN: No, actually the teacher sued the parents. He was a diminutive sort of chap — Indo Chinese, I believe — and the child you mentioned was in fact a twelve stone seventeen year old who was the Schools' Area boxing champion at the time.

AMANDA: You don't like your job then?

JOHN: Well, it lacks a certain savagery, but on ne whole I suppose it appeals to my basic animal instinct.

AMANDA: I'm teaching now, by the way.

JOHN: By the way of where?

AMANDA: I mean incidentally. I'm a relief.

JOHN: Really? Well, I'm glad you're a relief to somebody.

AMANDA: *(not amused)* Yes. I think I'll use the bathroom, if you don't mind.

JOHN: Of course. *(taking her to the door)* Up the stairs, first right.

AMANDA: Thank you. *(exits)*

JOHN: *(after a pause)* Another drink, Frank?

FRANK: Cheers. *(JOHN takes his glass and refills at the trolley)* Thank you. *(little pause)* We live in Surrey.

JOHN: Oh?

FRANK: Yes. Camberley.

JOHN: Oh.

FRANK: Yes. Probably get a fair price for it when we sell up.

JOHN: Good. Is that likely to be soon?

FRANK: Oh no. When we retire.

JOHN: Ah. Or perhaps when Amanda has finished her quest for old flames and decides to move on to another patch?

FRANK: *(after a pause)* She doesn't make a habit of this, you know?

JOHN: But you don't mind the odd one or two?

FRANK: Well, no. Why should I?

JOHN: Why should you indeed. Well, that's all right then.

FRANK: *(after a pause)* Actually, Amanda's never quite forgotten that day you stood her up.

JOHN: Yes, well I'm afraid I've never quite remembered it.

FRANK: It's been a cross for me to bear all these years. And when your letter appeared, well, of course, that was it. *(little pause)* Still, when you two knew each other, all that time ago, I suppose . . . .

JOHN: Yes?

FRANK: Well, I mean, from what you said earlier, I suppose you and Amanda were . . . . well, just kids really.

JOHN: Oh, quite young, yes.

FRANK: I thought so. It was platonic then?

JOHN: *(as if to put* FRANK'S *mind at rest)* Good God, no. Nothing like that.

FRANK: Oh?

JOHN: I can't even clearly remember what the attraction was. I expect it was just the sex. Anyway, we've been through all that now, so there's no need to worry, is there?

FRANK: She's a very determined woman.

JOHN: Yes, I would say so.

FRANK: *(after a little pause)* Your name, naturally, has been a household word since your letter appeared. In fact, I became quite curious to see you myself.

JOHN: Yes, I see.

FRANK: Do you?

JOHN: Pardon?

FRANK: Do you see? Do you know what it's like to live in someone's shadow? I don't suppose that your wife has any such shadows to cast over you, eh? In fact, I'm sure you were both quite made for each other and have no doubt lived blissfully together for many years. I don't suppose you've ever given a thought to old Amanda, nor would you have done to me, had you ever been even remotely aware of my existence. *(little pause)* But you see, I've been pain-

fully aware of yours — not just since your clever letter in
Times Ed. — oh, no — Amanda's goaded me before about
you — and I've been quite looking forward to this opportunity of meeting you face to face.

JOHN: *(after a little pause)* Well, Frank, I'm flattered.

FRANK: Yes. I've quite looked forward to breaking your neck.
(Makes movement forward towards JOHN, *as* AMANDA
returns)

AMANDA: I hope you two are getting on?

JOHN: Yes. Famously. *(pause)* Let me get you another drink.

AMANDA: Thank you. *(*JOHN *moves to the trolley.)* You have
children then, John?

JOHN: Just the one.

AMANDA: Boy or girl?

JOHN: *(after a pause)* A boy.

AMANDA: *(taking drink)* Thank you. Is he like you?

JOHN: We argue about the same things, yes.

AMANDA: Oh. *(pause)* I'm sorry I missed your wife, I really
did feel that she resented my visit yesterday.

JOHN: Good God, no.

AMANDA: As long as you're sure.

JOHN: Good God, no.

AMANDA: You're not sure then?

JOHN: Not entirely.

AMANDA: How do you mean?

JOHN: I mean I'm not entirely sure whether I'm sure that Helen
resented your visit yesterday, but I expect you did your
best.

AMANDA: Now that's not fair, John.

JOHN: No, I don't suppose it is absolutely fair, but then you
see, Helen's left me and that's not fair either.

AMANDA: Left you! *(pause)* I really don't know what to say.

JOHN: Most of it has been said already, so I shouldn't worry
because I really don't want to hear it again.

AMANDA: But, surely . . . . you don't mean that my visit was
something to do with it?

JOHN: Oh, a mere contribution, really.

AMANDA: *(after a pause)* John, I'm sorry.

JOHN: Was that it?

AMANDA: Was that what?

JOHN: Was that what it was that you didn't know what to say?

AMANDA: I know it sounds inadequate but . . . . what are you going to do?

JOHN: When?

AMANDA: Well, now, tomorrow . . . . you must do something surely?

JOHN: The same as I've always done. Eat, drink and sleep, with a scattering of teaching here and there.

AMANDA: But your wife . . . .

JOHN: Yes, well, Helen never interfered with any of them before so it makes no difference. *(There is a pause)*

FRANK: I'll just go to the bathroom.

JOHN: First right, top of the stairs. *(FRANK exits)*

AMANDA: *(after a pause)* You don't seem too distressed about it, if you don't mind me saying.

JOHN: Well, as you've already said it I fail to see the point of asking whether or not I mind.

AMANDA: It was merely a figure of speech.

JOHN: Is that all it was? *(little pause)* No, I'm not distressed.

AMANDA: *(after a pregnant pause)* I had a friend once whose husband left her. Poor girl was distraught about it, tears everywhere, couldn't eat, you know the sort of thing. Anyway, she assured me that it could be sorted out. *(little pause)* One night I was at her house, God it was pathetic, and she was saying how things would be back to normal again, etc. etc. — next day she gassed herself. I kept her company as much as I could but it was all too much for her.

JOHN: Which, your company or her husband leaving her?

AMANDA: That's unkind.

JOHN: Probably. Anyway, I'm not the suicidal type.

AMANDA: Oh, I wasn't drawing parallels. *(FRANK returns)*

JOHN: Would you say I was the suicidal type, Frank?

FRANK: I beg your pardon?

JOHN: Me. Suicidal. Am I the type?

FRANK: I don't know. Should you be?

JOHN: Only according to my bank statement. Are you?

FRANK: I've never tried it, no.

JOHN: No, but then those that have are very seldom the type that do. I knew someone once who tried it four times, which as you see proves that he wasn't very good at it, although it

certainly wasn't through lack of practise. Bear that in mind,
Frank.

FRANK: What?

JOHN: That suicides are not always as fatal as they may seem.

FRANK: If this is your attempt at being funny I really don't
see —

JOHN: That's quite all right, Frank, because you're not supposed
to. *(a pause follows)*

AMANDA: You're coping all right then, John?

JOHN: Under the circumstances, yes. And you? You and Frank, I
mean? No arguments or other complications?

AMANDA: Oh, no. Frank and I have always had an understanding.

JOHN: Jolly good. Any children?

AMANDA: No, that's part of the understanding. Oh, we have
the occasional cross word, of course, but on the whole, no
great mishaps.

JOHN: Well that sounds like an excellent arrangement.

FRANK: *(with intent)* Yes, it does, doesn't it.

JOHN: *(as if he had forgotten of* FRANK's *existence)* I beg
your pardon?

FRANK: What exactly have you got against the arrangement
of our marriage?

JOHN: What?

FRANK: Your tone.

JOHN: Tone?

FRANK: Is obviously one of derision and has been since we
arrived. So, come on, let's hear what you've got to say.

JOHN: Really, Frank, I've nothing whatsoever to say about
your marriage. No reason for criticism, no grounds for com-
plaint, I really don't see what you're getting at, old boy.

FRANK: I can smell your condescending, self-satisfied tone
from here, so let's hear it, shall we?

JOHN: Look, what is all this talk of tones all of a sudden? I
mean, Good God, Frank, old sport, first you offer to fight
me because I happen to be happily married, then you go
on about smelling my tone when I won't insult you because
you're happily married as well, I mean, I don't see where
my tone comes into it all, Good God.

AMANDA: What do you mean, he offered to fight you?

JOHN: Oh, you were conveniently out of the room at the time, but it's all settled now.

AMANDA: Frank? Whatever for?

FRANK: A matter of principle, Amanda.

AMANDA: Principle? I know your principles, Frank, and I fail to see any reason for picking fights with my friends.

JOHN: Really, Amanda, no blood has been spilt, no harm done and we're all friends again, so there's no cause for concern.

AMANDA: But all the same, John, Frank's behaviour has been quite –

JOHN: Frank's behaviour has been admirable inasmuch as he hasn't yet managed to provoke an unpleasant scene so let's keep it that way, shall we? *(a pause follows)*

AMANDA: You show incredible restraint, John.

JOHN: This far, yes.

AMANDA: Was that meant for me?

JOHN: Not necessarily, but let's keep open minds.

AMANDA: *(after a pause)* You love your wife then, John?

JOHN: Frequently. Why?

AMANDA: Well, under the circumstances, you've kept your anxiety remarkably under control. I mean, for Heaven's sake, don't let our presence here make you feel obliged to cover up the tremendous strain you must be under.

JOHN: I give you my word, Amanda, I haven't tried to cover up for it, nor felt obliged to.

AMANDA: Perhaps you'd like us to go now?

JOHN: Well, I must confess – *(The front door closes.* HELEN *enters.)* Helen! *(little pause)* I'm afraid you've missed tea. Yesterday's as well, in fact.

HELEN: I won't be stopping. I've just come to collect a few things, so don't let me interrupt.

JOHN: Oh, Amanda and Frank were just leaving. I believe you've met Amanda?

HELEN: *(coldly)* Yes.

AMANDA: Helen, I think you misunderstood my visit yesterday –

HELEN: No. No, I don't think so.

JOHN: This is Amanda's husband, Frank.

FRANK: Hello.

HELEN: Hello. I really can't stop, John, I've got plenty of things to do.

JOHN: You're going to see this charade through to the finish then?

HELEN: Just that far, yes.

AMANDA: Helen, John and I haven't seen each other for fifteen years.

HELEN: Really?

JOHN: Twenty. Not for over twenty years, in fact, nor, probably for another twenty.

AMANDA: I don't think my appearance yesterday was quite what you thought, Helen.

HELEN: Oh? It was a business call then?

JOHN: Helen, you're being deliberately childish.

HELEN: Am I? Then it makes a pleasant change from you being deliberately childish, doesn't it?

JOHN: I fail to see what all the dramatics are about.

HELEN: No. No. I don't think you do. *(exits. There is a pause)*

AMANDA: I'm sorry, John.

JOHN: Whatever for, Good God? I mean, I may have lost my wife, and your role in that may not be without significance, my son might well hate me and may soon be joining the ranks of the criminal underworld, on top of which I may well have lost my job as well as the friendship of my best friend, but the situation is not without merit inasmuch as things can only get better. *(little pause)* Wouldn't you agree? *(The front doorbell rings.)* Excuse me. *(exits. A short pause follows, during which voices are heard in the hall.* JOHN *returns with* JACK*)* Come in, Jack; this is Amanda and Frank. You might remember Amanda actually, we had a thing going either before or after my marriage, we can't decide which.

JACK: Oh? Pleased to meet you again.

AMANDA: Hello.

FRANK: Hello.

JACK: *(to* AMANDA*)* Face does look familiar. Haven't I seen you in the pub recently?

JOHN: Oh, that's quite likely, Jack. The mysterious lady you mentioned the other day was none other than Amanda.

JACK: I thought so. *(pause)* Is Helen around?

JOHN: I believe she's upstairs. She might pop in to say hello, possibly goodbye.

JACK: Oh? She's going away then?

JOHN: That will depend largely on what she says if and when she pops in to say it.

JACK: *(clearly puzzled)* Oh. *(pause)* Anyway, good news, John.

JOHN: Really? I'd come to believe there was no such thing anymore.

JACK: Well this should restore your faith; you're not having an affair with Angela.

JOHN: *(pause; impassive)* I'm not? Well, Jack, I must say you don't know what a load off my mind that is. But that's hardly good news. I mean, it's undoubtedly good, and it may well be news to you, but it certainly isn't to me.

JACK: No, I suppose not. But the point is that nobody is. Having an affair with her, I mean. I dashed straight round to tell you. *(*HELEN *enters)*

JOHN: Ah, Helen. Jack's just dashed round to tell me I'm not having an affair with his wife.

HELEN: Oh?

JACK: Yes. Sorry about all the fuss . . . . you know.

HELEN: How did you find out?

JACK: Well, I was bloody stupid really. That night after I came here making a fool of myself I went home and had a great big scene following which we both sulked for a couple of days, then tonight we sat down and talked it out. It was bloody yoga after all. *(pause)* Anyway . . . . sorry.

JOHN: Good God, don't apologize, there's really no need. I mean, we've all had a bit of fun at my expense, haven't we?

JACK: But at least let me —

JOHN: No, I insist — after all, you've all played your parts with great purpose, and tempered your abuse with a degree of humour — you, Jack, have dashed in and out of my house on the one hand to accuse me of having an affair with your wife and on the other to apologize because I'm not, implying that you had hoped I was after all. Amanda has appeared from the past apparently to make good for the time that I stood her up twenty years ago and has seen fit to bring along her husband who in turn is itching to break my skull, the reason for which seems momentarily obscure, whilst you, Helen, seem strangely discontent with walking out of my life merely once, but appear to be in the throes of doing so again tonight — *(pause)* Yes, I think you've all done rather well. *(There is a pause during which nobody knows quite what to say.* JOHN *pours himself a drink.)*

AMANDA: Well, I think we ought to be going, Frank.

FRANK: Yes, I think so.

AMANDA: *(collecting her handbag, etc.)* I really am very sorry, Helen. *(pause)* Well, we can see ourselves out. Goodbye, John.

JOHN: Until we meet again.

AMANDA: Yes. *(Exit* AMANDA *and* FRANK.*)*

JACK: I'd best be off as well, John.

JOHN: Don't take anything I've said to heart, Jack, because if you start paying attention to anything I say it could spoil a friendship that has spanned more years than I can remember.

JACK: Sure. *(pause)* I don't know where I got the idea about you and Angela.

JOHN: I'm afraid your wife's affairs, or lack of them, have never been of much interest to me.

JACK: No. Anyway, I'll be off. Bye, Helen.

HELEN: Goodbye, Jack.

JACK: Yes. I'll see myself out. *(exits)*
(There is a pause)

JOHN: And then there were two. *(pause)* Jennifer's here.

HELEN: What?

JOHN: Oh, not at the moment. But if you hang on a minute you might catch her.

HELEN: How has she been?

JOHN: Oh, wonderfully morbid. But she has served a certain nuisance value which has seemed to fit in with the general run of things, and her redeeming feature of course is that she makes Jack and Amanda and Frank and all the rest look almost essential.

HELEN: And me? Does she make me look almost essential as well?

JOHN: Well, I mean, under the circumstances —

HELEN: I realize I've been incredibly naive.

JOHN: Well —

HELEN: I have. I came here tonight not to collect my things but to bring them back. It was only when I saw that woman here . . . .

JOHN: Yes. Amanda, that would be. *(pause)* Where have you been? *(sitting down on sofa)*

HELEN: Round the corner. The Gateway Hotel. *(sits, left.)*

JOHN: What's it like?

HELEN: Probably only twice as bad as you think it is.

JOHN: Oh. Good.

HELEN: Where's Peter?

JOHN: Oh, he's gone out . . . . somewhere. May or may not be back, I think were his precise words, although they were uttered as he was half way through the door.

HELEN: Oh. *(pause)* Anyway, I'm sorry.

JOHN: Yes. *(Pause)* Would you like a drink?

HELEN: Yes, please. *(JOHN gets up and pours a drink)* Thank you. No harm's been done then?

JOHN: *(sitting)* No. We've had a breather, that's all. *(pause)* In a way I'm quite grateful.

HELEN: It *has* served a purpose then?

JOHN: Inasmuch as Jennifer is all set to leave first thing in the morning, Amanda has been nicely despatched back from whence she came, and plans to demolish a certain college of education have fallen apart at the seams, which would appear to be a very good place for them to fall apart at, whilst I'm pleasantly drunk. *(pause)* Yes, I suppose in the balance it's all been worthwhile. *(The lights fade slowly to blackout, then:)*

CURTAIN

PERSONAL PROPERTIES

JOHN: Cigarettes, Lighter (In jacket on chair; Act II)

HELEN: (Act II) Handbag, Wedding Ring

ADRIAN: Afghan type coat, patchwork shoulder
                 bag containing books etc.

JENNIFER: Travelling case, handbag

COLLINS: Bulging brief case, spectacles.

AMANDA: Handbag, light overcoat.

LIGHTING PLOT

A Living Room.

ACT 1   Evening. About 10.00 pm.
    Overall effect of an autumn evening.
    Page 27 . . . . HELEN : 'Anything'
    Pause;   then, BLACKOUT

ACT II
    Scene One.   Afternoon
    Overall effect of an autumn afternoon
    Page 51 . . . . JENNIFER exits
    Pause;   then, BLACKOUT

    Scene Two   Evening.   About 7.00 pm.
    Overall effect of evening
    Page 75 . . . . . JOHN :' . . . . . it's all been worthwhile'
    Pause;   then, FADE to BLACKOUT

NEW PLAYWRIGHTS' NETWORK

This exciting project was launched in January 1972. Each year many of the major county and borough libraries have agreed to accept a quota of new, full length stage plays which will be included in their central collections for use by A.D.S. for play reading purposes with a view to possible performances. Each play published has been approved by a distinguished panel of readers who have specialised knowledge of amateur theatre requirements. Our aim is to publish high quality plays to enable N.P.N. to compete successfully with the belated products from the West End. N.P.N. offers the best package deal ever made available to the talented struggling-playwright. Keep in touch with your local library!

SPECIAL NOTE to Amateur Dramatic Societies.

Triple Bill Presentation

These will cut your performance fees to enable you to use and develop your resources to much greater advantage.

NEW PLAYS

Your support will give much needed encouragement to the many talented playwrights.